CW00369874

Purnululu National Park

Western Australia

Western Australia covers an area of 2.5 million square kilometres almost the same as the whole of Europe. It is not only the largest State in Australia, it is also the least populated with just over 1.9 million people of whom 1.3 million reside in the capital city, Perth. Visitors to this vast State often comment on how few people they have encountered on the country roads whilst touring on their holiday. This small gift book shows how varied and beautiful Western Australia can be and will hold many fond memories for those who have enjoyed their travels through this vast State and provide inspiration for those yet to visit.

North of Cue

CONTENTS

Perth city skyline

P e r t h

Is she real–she certainly is. Miriam of the Kinetic Theatre Company enthrals the many visitors here at London Court.

Perth is one of the most isolated capital cities in the world. The nearest major city, Adelaide in South Australia, is over 2800 kms away. Perth is noted for its Mediterranean climate with mild winters and warm, sunny summers. Combine this with a casual lifestyle and generally clean environment and one has a city that is both relaxing and welcoming. Almost continuous sandy beaches line the adjacent coastline with the peaceful island of Rottnest just a short distance away. All the facilities of any major city can be found here in Perth but, unlike many capital cities, the peace and quiet of the countryside are only a short journey away.

The Noongar people have hunted and gathered food on the banks of the Swan River for thousands of years. In 1829 the first European settlement was set up under the leadership of Captain James Stirling. From these humble beginnings, Perth has developed in under 200 years into a city of beauty comparable to any other modern capital city in the world.

It's hard to imagine that the temporary wildflower displays are erected and dismantled in the just two weeks for the spring Wildflower Festival in Kings Park.

The city from King's Park

The Brass Monkey Hotel

The Swan Bells in Barrack Square

Over page—Longreach Bay Rottnest Island

People dining at Cicerello's in Fremantle Harbour

Fremantle

Fremantle has a character all of its own. The fine old buildings have been faithfully restored and the markets, cappuccino strip and harbour restaurants offer the visitor a relaxed, inviting atmosphere. There are many reminders of the early colonial days such as the Fremantle Prison, the Round House, the Maritime Museum and the Fremantle Arts Centre. Set on the mouth of the Swan River, Fremantle is still the major working port for Western Australia moving many millions of tonnes of cargo a year. The bustle of the harbour sits comfortably with the historic atmosphere and fine buildings. For many visitors, Fremantle is one of the major highlights of their stay in this large State, with so much to see and do.

Cappuccino strip

Opposite—A talented street artist holds the attention of a large crowd outside the Sail and Anchor Hotel, Fremantle

A walking trail in the tall Karri forest

South West

Weather patterns are more variable in the South West which has, generally, a wetter climate than the Perth region. The additional rainfall is reflected in the beautiful tall Karri and Jarrah forests. These 60 metre tall trees tower above the many country roads that wander through the South West. The southern coastline has a wild, windswept feel, even though most of the year it is bathed in sunshine. Even if the visitor has only limited time in Western Australia a visit to the South West is a must.

Opposite—A spring fed stream at Ellensbrook (Mokidup) near Margaret River

Verticordias in full bloom east of Hyden

Wildflowers of the South West

The South West is one of the botanical wonders of the world, with over 9000 species of flowering plants. Travelling from early August to mid-October will reveal a wonderland of plants, particularly in the Stirling Ranges and the Fitzgerald River National Park.

A road side verge in the Ravensthorpe Range

Wandoo woodland, Stirling Range National Park

Mermaid Point near Cheyne Beach and Cutleaf Banksia *(Banksia praemorsa)*

Over page—Waychinicup Bay

Elephant Rocks, Williams Bay

Hellfire Bay, Cape Le Grand National Park

Looking out to the Southern Ocean from Twilight Beach Road, Esperance

Dave Evans Bicentennial Tree near Pemberton

Walking on the Ancient Empire trail near Walpole

Albany

Although Perth is the capital city of Western Australia, Albany was actually settled three and a half years earlier. Its fine harbour made a safe haven for the early sailing ships. Initially a military garrison was established then, over the years, the town became a major supply centre for the region. It makes an ideal base from which to travel to other South West areas. Albany itself has beautiful beaches and wonderful historic buildings. The port has an historic whaling station but nowadays, whales visit the area and are spotted from hilltop vantage points.

The Gap, Torndirrup National Park

The 'Amity', Albany
Opposite—York Street, Albany

The Stirling Ranges

The Stirling Ranges rise to 1073m (3500 ft) with Bluff Knoll being the highest peak in the range. There are walks to the various summits and in spring, the wildflower displays are some of the

Wildflowers on Baby Barnett Hill, Stirling Range National Park

Stirling Range

finest in the State. A journey along the Stirling Range Drive will give the visitor an excellent opportunity to witness the great variety of plant life as well as the spectacular scenery.

Bluff Knoll, Stirling Range

Some of the most picturesque countryside in the State is found between Cape Leeuwin and Cape Naturaliste. The region has so much to offer the traveller including famous wineries, some with wine tasting centres, great restaurants and excellent art and wood craft galleries. The coastline is spectacular, with some of the best surfing beaches in Australia. A drive along Caves Road offers numerous beach locations, all with their separate bays and wonderful sandy beaches. Set behind the limestone coastline are some beautiful caves that are open to the public and well worth a visit.

One of the many surfing beaches near Margaret River

Voyager Estate, Margaret River

Wheatbelt

The wheatbelt region was once covered in open woodland. It has largely been cleared for agriculture but there are many reserves where the visitor can find peace and quiet. Many people visit the various granite outcrops, the most popular being Wave Rock, on the eastern edge of the wheatbelt, near Hyden.

Salmon Gums on a wheatbelt road

Wave Rock, near Hyden

York

Established in 1830, York is set on the banks of the Avon River just under 100 km from Perth. The township contains a wealth of early colonial buildings, most faithfully restored. The town is noted for its Jazz Festival and Vintage Car Rallies and boasts one of the finest vintage car museums in the world.

Settlers House, York

Town Hall, York

Goldfields

The Eastern Goldfields are located 600 km east of Perth. There were many goldrushes throughout Australia. In 1892, Arthur Bailey and Bill Ford rode from where Coolgardie now stands into Southern Cross with 555 oz of gold which led to the mighty gold rush days of the late 1890s. The region centred around Kalgoorlie has produced vast amounts of gold for over 100 years and gold is still being taken from the vast super pits and small mines of the Eastern Goldfields.

York Hotel, Kalgoorlie

Eucalypts at dusk, Goldfields

The giant "Super Pit" on the Golden Mile

The old headframes of the early mining days, Kalgoorlie

The Exchange Hotel, Kalgoorlie

Hannan Street, Kalgoorlie

Kalgoorlie, Boulder & Coolgardie

These towns show wonderful examples of early colonial architecture. The number of Hotels that were built in the late 1890s is staggering and many are still in use today. After Bailey and Ford discovered gold in the Coolgardie area, three Irishmen, Patrick Hannan, Tom Flanagan and Daniel Shea found gold in the area where the great super pit is now located on the outskirts of Kalgoorlie. Literally thousands of men came to the region looking for gold. Before the Perth to Kalgoorlie railway line was constructed, many arrived in Albany by boat, made their way by trains to York and then walked an incredible distance of 500 km to the Eastern Goldfields.

The Marvel Bar Hotel, Coolgardie

Thelma Higgins father kept old mining machinery parts. Over the years the collection grew with more Goldfields memorabilia being added as the years went by.

Nullarbor

The Nullarbor is a vast limestone karst plateau covering 250,000 square kilometres. North of the east-west highway are areas with literally no trees, only samphire and grass plains. The area was once an ancient seabed which became a barrier for vegetation types between the eastern and western states. Some of the longest subterranean caves in the world are found under this vast plateau.

Delisser Sandunes, Eucla

The Nullarbor Plain

North of Cue

Mid West

The Mid West has much to offer the traveller—the limestone columns of the Pinnacles, the picturesque Benedictine township of New Norcia and numerous National Parks noted for their wonderful wildflower displays. Sheep stations stretch from the World Heritage area of Shark Bay all the way to the desert country and many offer home stay accommodation; a great way to experience outback Australia.

The Pinnacles, Nambung National Park

The Pinnacles

The Pinnacles are located in Nambung National Park, 245 km by road north of Perth. They are tall columns of soft limestone which were created by water leaching through the soils and subsequently exposed by wind erosion.

Mullewa

Opposite is the Church of Our Lady of Mount Carmel and Saints' Peter and Paul founded by the famous parish priest Monseigneur John Hawes with the help of local farmers and parishioners.

New Norcia

This unique settlement just north of Perth was founded by Spanish Benedictine monks in 1846. The monastery and churches are still in use to this day and visitors to New Norcia find the peace and tranquillity very uplifting. It has one of the best religious art collections in Australia.

The Church of Our Lady of Mount Carmel and Saints Peter and Paul

The Benedictine community museum, art gallery and the old covent school, New Norcia

Kalbarri

This picturesque town is located at the mouth of the Murchison River estuary and adjacent to Kalbarri National Park which is famous for its wildflowers in spring and summer.

Murchison River Gorge, Kalbarri National Park

Monkey Mia

Here in the clear waters of Shark Bay visitors can experience the unequalled pleasure of seeing wild Bottlenose Dolphins coming into the shallow bay at Monkey Mia of their own free choice.

Bottlenose Dolphins paying a visit to Monkey Mia

South of New Norcia

Wildflowers of the Mid West

The South West and the Mid West possess the largest variety of plant species in Australia. In the Mid West the Verticordias, or Featherflowers, really come into their own, dominating much of the countryside in late spring and early summer.

Everlastings near Paynes Find

Morrison Feather flower *(verticordia nitens)* Moore River

Verticordia monadelpha, Kalbarri

Pilbara

Often known as the North West, this region has some of the most spectacular scenery in the State, particularly in the National Parks such as Karijini, Mount Augustus, Cape Range and the Kennedy Range National Parks. Those who love fishing or diving will find Ningaloo Reef a very rewarding place to visit.

Fortescue Falls, Karijini National Park

Typical north west river after the cyclonic rains have long gone
Opposite—Sunset in the Hamersley Range

Mining in the Pilbara

Mining gives employment to a huge work force and rewards the State with substantial income. A visit to an open cut mine site, like Mount Newman, is an awesome experience in terms of the dimensions of the open pit, size of the equipment and volume of earth moved. Safety regulations are very important and the whole mining operation runs with total efficiency.

Mount Newman mine

The super pit–Mount Newman mine

The North West gas project near Karratha

Dale Gorge–Karijini National Park
Opposite—Dawn in the Hamersley Range

Chichester Range

Giant granite boulders, south of Port Hedland

A well used saddle

The shearing shed

Station country

Life on the sheep or cattle stations is seen by many visitors as "the real Australia" even though most Australians now live in cities. The lifestyle on the stations is often hard and the financial rewards few, yet there is a romance about outback life which nothing else can replace.

Many sheep and cattle stations offer the traveller accommodation and sometimes guided tours. There is no better way to get to know Australians than to stay with these fine, hard working people.

Glen's at home on the big north west cattle stations.

The Chichester Range

Near Circular Pool, Karijini National Park

Big country, big vehicles–a road train in the Hamersley Range

The majestic and remote Rudhall River (*Kandimalal*) National Park

Bell Gorge off the Gibb River Road

Kimberley

One of the last outback frontiers of Australia, the Kimberley has a character all of its own. The fine country and wonderful people make a great combination and the traveller will sense the unique spirit of this remote land. The drive from Broome in the west or Kununurra in the east will take you through historic Kimberley towns and wonderful open plains. Both are thriving towns with lots to do for the visitor. Those who drive down the Gibb River Road will pass through some of the most magnificent scenery in the State. Rock pools, paperbark lined rivers, rugged ranges, gorges and large cattle stations will greet the visitor. When the southern regions of Australia are experiencing their coldest weather, in the north the sun will normally be shining, and with daytime temperatures between 27°C and 30°C it is the ideal place to escape the winter chill.

Geikie Gorge

Cable Beach, Broome

Broome

Once one of the pearling capitals of the world, Broome still has a thriving pearl industry. It certainly is a town for the sun-seeking tourist with Cable Beach being a "Mecca" for the traveller. Whether it is lazing in the warm winter sun or riding camels into the sunset, there will be lots to do here. The Broome township retains much of its past life, such as the old Court House which is still in use. The extensive Japanese cemetery has numerous black granite tombstones bearing the names of the many Japanese pearl divers who lost their lives through diving tragedies or in one of the many tropical cyclones that have hit the far north coastline.

Camels at sunset, Cable Beach

The Bungle Bungle Range, Purnululu National Park

Cape Leveque 195 km north of Broome

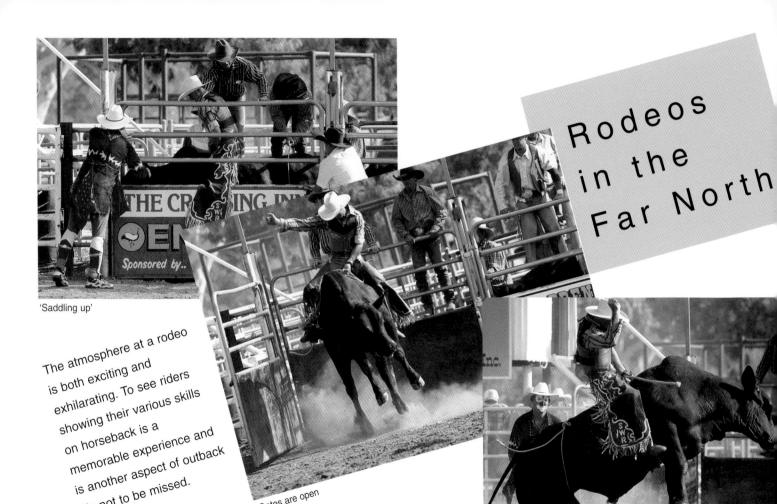

'Saddling up'

The atmosphere at a rodeo is both exciting and exhilarating. To see riders showing their various skills on horseback is a memorable experience and is another aspect of outback life not to be missed.

Gates are open

The real hard work begins. Only one hand is allowed to hold onto the reins in buck and bull riding.

Station people enjoying the Camp Drafting event, Fitzroy Crossing

Saddling up

His mum said he has been given a new hat, but prefers his old one.

Holding the Culture

In a predominantly western society, it is not easy for Aboriginal people to keep their culture. Men like Donny Woolagoodja of the *Worora* tribe at *Mowanjum* community in the north west Kimberley are certainly keeping it. Many of us were privileged to see Donny's *Wanjina* graphics and concepts displayed in the Opening Ceremony of the 2000 Sydney Olympic Games. The *Worora*, *Ngarinyin* and *Wunumbul* people at *Mowanjum* as well as countless other Aboriginal tribal groups throughout Australia are trying hard to hold onto their ancestral stories— may they long remain.

Donny Woolagoodja with one of his stunning *Wandjina* paintings

Passing down *'stories'* to the children is important at *Mowanjum*, Kimberley